Knitting

This edition published in 2012
By SpiceBox™
12171 Horseshoe Way,
Richmond, BC,
Canada V7A 4V4

First published in 2009
Copyright © SpiceBox™ 2009

ISBN 10: 1-927010-51-9
ISBN 13: 978-1-927010-51-8

CEO and Publisher: Ben Lotfi
Author: Astor Tsang
Creative Director: Garett Chan
Art Director: Christine Covert
Designer: Mell D'Clute, Kirsten Reddecopp
Production: James Badger, Mell D'Clute
Sourcing: Janny Lam
Photography: Devin Karringten
Models: Arlen Tom, Jacqueline Mae Boudreau
Makeup Artist: Natalee Fera
Stylist: Maeve Doyle

For more SpiceBox products and information, visit our website:
www.spicebox.ca

Manufactured in China

1 3 5 7 9 10 8 6 4 2

Table of Contents

Getting Started _____ 5
   Yarn
   Tools
   Reading Yarn Labels
   Choosing Yarn and Yarn Substitutions
   Winding a Ball Off Skein
   Measurement
How-to-Knit Basics _____ 8
   Slip knot
   Casting On
   Knit Stitch
   Purl Stitch
   Tension
   Knit and Purl Combinations
   Reading Your Work
   Turning
   Casting Off
Finishing _____ 15
   Blocking
   Sewing
   Darning Ends

Beyond the Basics _____ 17
   Reading a Pattern
   Knitting on Gauge
   Transferring Stitches
   Ending Yarn
   Joining Yarn
   Increasing – Make One and Yarn Over
   Decreasing – Knit 2 Together
   Casting On Mid-Row – Backward Loop Method
   Buttonhole
   Design
   Stitch Patterns
   Counting Stitches
Projects _____ 24
   Scarf
   Slouch Hat
   Ribbed Tube Top
   Top-Down Shrug Cardigan
Appendix _____ 36
Glossary _____ 38
How to Determine Your Size _____ 39

Foreword

When SpiceBox approached me to write a knitting book, I was thrilled. I thought, "What a great opportunity to share my love for knitting."

For almost ten years now, I have taught knitting to beginners at various community centers in Vancouver, BC. I have developed a teaching style that is all my own.

One thing I have learned—the hard way, I might add—is to assume that nothing is obvious to my students. I find when I am problem-solving for either the students in my classes or customers at the local yarn store I work at, most of the frustration comes from the instructions making an assumption of knowledge the knitter should have, but doesn't. I am always shocked at how many knitting instructions are assumed to be obvious. In this book, by constantly explaining concepts, I hope to present a tool for beginners to become confident, self-taught knitters.

Warning: Knitting is addictive, and by picking up this book, you have just been infected!

Enjoy the ride.

Astor

Getting Started

One thing to keep in mind about the craft of knitting is that the terms used are sometimes confusing. One term can mean many different things depending on the context in which it is written. Throughout the book, I will try to clarify the few terms we use for knitting. As well, an appendix and a glossary can be found at the end of the book to help you along the way.

YARN

Yarn is a continuous strand made up of fibers used for knitting. Yarn can be made from any materials—natural, synthetic, or a combination of the two—and describes all the varying materials we knit with. The term "wool" refers specifically to yarn made from the fiber from sheep or other woolly animals. The term "string" is rarely used for knitting, although technically you can knit with string.

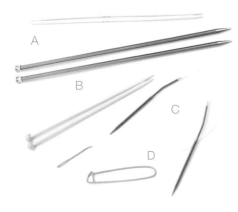

Types of needles: A. Double-pointed, B. Straight, C. Circular, D. Stitch Holder

TOOLS

To knit, all you need are two needles and yarn. The most common materials for needles are plastic, metal, and wood (usually bamboo, but can get as exotic as rosewood and ebony). Needles come in three common shapes or forms: straight, circular and double-pointed. I recommend that, as a beginner, you learn to knit with straight bamboo needles.

READING YARN LABELS

Each ball of yarn has a label called the ball band. The ball band not only identifies the yarn, but includes important information for the knitter. Although some of the information is quite obvious, like yarn material content and washing instructions, there is some other information that I would like to touch upon.

Yarn weight vs. yardage – When you are comparing quantities of yarn, ball to ball, look at the yardage. In other words, how long is the yarn if you unravel the ball? The weight, on the other hand, can be misleading. Some yarns are just heavier than others, but do not give you more material to knit with. For example, one 1 ¾ ounce (50-gram) ball of 100% silk yarn has 136 yards (124 m) while the same weight of bamboo-wool blend yarn has only 104 yards (95 m). In this example, you have more silk than bamboo-wool to knit with.

Dye lots – The dye lot is usually the stamped number—not the printed number—on the ball band. When yarn is dyed in a factory, it is done in batches. The dye lot identifies which batch the yarn was colored in. Although yarn can have the same color and style numbers, shades can vary between batches. This is because dyes can be affected by outside factors like humidity or by what color was used just before. To maintain a consistent look in your project, you'll want yarn that was all dyed in the same batch.

Gauge of the yarn – This is a measurement of how thick the yarn strand is, usually shown on the ball band by a square diagram which indicates how many stitches are knitted in 4 inches (10 cm). Sometimes if the diagram isn't present, the ball band will just say the number of stitches in 4 inches (10 cm). Some ball bands only list the number of stitches in one inch, in which case, multiply that number by four to get the industry standard number.

Note: The higher the gauge number, the thinner the yarn will be. There are also names for each set of gauges (see Appendix on page 36 for the chart). For example, a 22-gauge, or double knitting (DK) weight, is finer than a 16-gauge yarn, or Aran weight.

CHOOSING YARN AND YARN SUBSTITUTIONS

When it comes to choosing yarn for your projects, my first advice is to go to your local yarn store (LYS). You'll not only find a great yarn selection, but the staff at the stores are all knowledgeable and can provide you with the help you need.

There are two approaches to take in choosing yarn. You can either choose your yarn first, then decide what you are going to make out of it, or you can choose your project first, then decide on the yarn.

I suggest beginners choose a project first. The staff at the yarn store can then help you select the appropriate yarn for the project you've chosen.

If the project you choose specifies a particular yarn available in the store, your job is easy. You just need to select a color. Sometimes, however, you will have to make a yarn substitution. This is because, with the huge amount of yarn available, a yarn store cannot carry them all. Also, some older patterns may specify yarn that is no longer available. Some knitters try

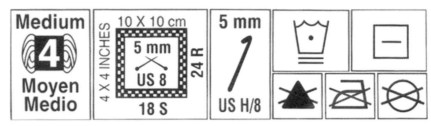

to find a particular yarn for sale online, but I personally like to go to a store to see and feel my yarn before I buy it.

Whichever way you buy your yarn, keep in mind the following factors:

Weight – How thick is the yarn that you need? Match the gauge of the yarn specified in the pattern to the yarn you select. Choosing a yarn of a different gauge can result in drastically different results.

Fiber – Unlike weight, there is a little more flexibility in choosing a fiber for your project. If the pattern calls for a wool-cotton blend, then you may want to find another wool-cotton blend. But I like to experiment with different fiber options. A pattern for a cotton summer sweater can be transformed into a fall layer when you select a wool yarn instead.

Texture – Yarn comes in many textures including smooth, thick or thin, hand-spun look, bouclé, haze, etc. What you choose is up to you, but remember, if it's different from the yarn in the pattern, it can completely change the look of your project.

Color – Sometimes, the color will lead to the yarn selection. If you have a pumpkin orange sweater in mind, that may limit the selection of yarn to choose from. At the yarn store, you may also be introduced to variegated colored yarn (dyed into patches of different colors) and self-striping yarns (dyed into blended strips of color).

Cost – The fiber you choose will effect the cost of the project. For example, merino wool will be more expensive than other wools; thus you have to balance softness with cost.

WINDING A BALL OFF SKEIN

Often, when you purchase yarn, it will be in a skein (also called a "hank"). A skein is a length of yarn wound in a very large loose loop (Fig. 1a). Knitting with the yarn in a skein can result in a tangled mess. Instead, you'll want to wind the skein into a ball.

To start, untwist the skein to make a large circular loop. Then, if you have a friend to assist you, you can put the loop onto your friend's spread-out hands. Or, if no one is around, you can also place the loop onto the back of a chair. If the chair is able to spin, it's even better.

You'll see that the yarn is tied together either by waste yarn or by the same yarn as the skein. Once the loop is secure, untie or cut these temporary yarn fasteners and find the ends of the yarn for the skein. There should be one outside end (wrapping around on the outside of the skein) and one inside end. Take one end (usually the outside, but either will work) and hold it pointing down in the palm of your hand. Position your fingers in the trigger mode and wrap the yarn in a figure eight configuration between your finger and thumb (Fig. 1b). Wrap around your fingers ten times (Fig. 1c).

Carefully, take the pile of figure eights off your fingers, with the end of the yarn still sticking out (Fig. 1d). Fold the figure eights into a wad with a tail. Proceed to wrap the yarn from the skein around the wad you just made. Remember, as you wind the ball of yarn, keep the tail end free and accessible. This will give you the option to either pull from the outside or from the inside of the ball. Winding the ball is easy. Just make sure you keep twisting the ball around to distribute the yarn evenly. Also, do not wind the yarn too tight or it will stretch.

Sometimes you will come to a knot in the skein of yarn. This is because the yarn manufacturer may have had to join the yarn to make the skein. If you come across a knot, cut it and start a new ball.

MEASUREMENT

In this book, I will be using two forms of measurement. One uses a ruler or measuring tape, and the second uses your body for measurement. I use the body measurement method when I only need an approximate length of yarn and I don't have a long measuring tape on hand. Your body is always with you—you never forget to pack that into your knitting bag! When measuring with your body, one arm length is equal to the distance between the tip of your finger to your nose while your arm is outstretched. When I say "both arm length," I refer to the distance from the fingertip of one hand to the fingertip of the other while your arms are outstretched.

Winding Ball Off Skein

Fig. 1a

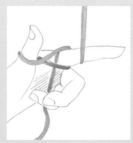

Fig. 1b

Fig. 1c

Fig. 1d

How-to-Knit Basics

A Note for Lefties:

It has always been my advice to left-handers to try knitting the right-handed way. My reasoning for this is that you use both hands for knitting anyway. Give the method described here a try before resorting to the left-handed method on page 36. The left-handed method may make reading patterns and learning more complicated stitches problematic.

START KNITTING!

The method of knitting described here is the English or American method, wherein you hold the yarn in your right hand while knitting. Some people also call it the "throw" method.

The method of knitting wherein you hold the yarn in your *left* hand is called the Continental, or "picking", method, but this will not be covered in this book.

SLIP KNOT

Begin by measuring a length of yarn. The length you need depends on how many stitches you are going to cast on. For example, if you are casting on less than 30 stitches, then you need only one arm-length of yarn. But if you are casting on 100 stitches, you may need two both-arm lengths. Whatever the number of stitches you cast on, the length of yarn is an approximation because there's no need

for exact measurement. But, as I tell my students, always estimate more, because if you run out of yarn, then you have to start all over again. Leftover yarn can be used for sewing.

At the measured point, create a loop by twisting or folding the yarn, making sure to leave enough to cast on your stitches. Take yarn from the ball end and thread it through the loop you just made, hooking your finger in the loop. Tighten by pulling both the ends of the yarn to make a slip knot. The size of the loop should be adjustable from the *ball side*. If not, you didn't take the loop of yarn from the ball side. Undo and try again.

CASTING ON

Casting on refers to putting stitches on your needle. There are many ways to cast on. *Vogue Knitting: The Ultimate Knitting Book* (Smith & Smith Books, 2002) demonstrates more than eleven different cast-on methods.

I teach what Vogue Knitting calls the "double cast-on" or the "long-tail cast-on" method. I feel this method gives the nicest looking stretchy edge and is the easiest to learn for a beginner. In my years of teaching, I've adapted this method for my students. The end results are the same, but the way it's done differs.

Here's how to do it:
1. Place the tail end on your left side, slip knot in the middle and the ball on your right side.

2. Put two needles together, side-to-side and parallel, with tips and ends together.

3. Point the needle tips away from you and slide the slip knot on. The knot should be under the needles with the tail end on your left, and the ball on your right. The slip knot counts as your first stitch.

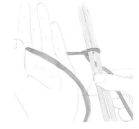

4. With the strand of yarn still in your right hand, hold the needles in your right hand.

5. Holding the tail end of the yarn in your left fist, palm facing down, rotate your wrist until it is palm up and the yarn forms a loop around your hand.

6. Open your fingers, in your palm will be a strand of yarn.

7. With your right hand, poke the needles under the yarn in your left hand, catching the loop. The needles should be pointing in the same direction as your fingers are pointing on your left hand.

8. Fold your left thumb over the needles to support them.

9. Still holding the yarn from the ball end, your right hand can let go of the needles.

10. With your right hand, swing the yarn out, around, and under the point of the needles, bringing it over the needles so that the yarn is back to the right side.

11. With your right hand, grab the needles again.

12. Releasing the thumb of your left hand from the needles, move the left hand up toward the end of the needles and flip the loop over the tips.

13. Take your left hand out of the loop of yarn.

14. Pull the tail end of the yarn tight around the needles. Then pull the ball end of the yarn in the other direction to make a neat knot around the needles. Don't worry about being too tight; the two needles allow for this.

You have just cast on a stitch. You should have two stitches now (the slip knot is one and the one you just made is the other). Each loop is considered a stitch. Now repeat steps 5 to 15.

Once you have cast on the number of stitches you desire, pull one needle out of the stitches. Tie the leftover tail end of yarn into a bobbin (you can do this by folding the tail in half once or twice and then tying it to itself) and let hang. This keeps the tail out of your way as you work. Place the ball of yarn on your right-hand side.

KNIT STITCH

Some beginners find that repeating a knitting rhyme helps them remember all the steps to knitting a stitch. You can find many knitting rhymes to help you. The most common one is:

*In through the front door,
Around the back,
Out through the window,
And off jumps Jack! (Waldorf)*

I. With your left hand, hold the needle with the stitches on it like a bicycle handlebar with the tip pointing to your right.

2. With your right hand, hold the empty needle with the tip pointing to your left. Your right hand can hold the needle either like a pencil or like a bicycle handlebar. Then, still holding the needle, grasp the yarn with your right hand.

3. Insert the tip of the empty needle into the first stitch, crossing below the left needle (Fig. 3a or 3b). In other words, insert the needle from the bottom right of the loop, into the loop, coming out of the top left.

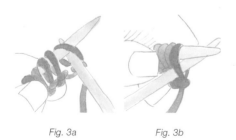

Fig. 3a   Fig. 3b

4. Using the left hand to hold the two needles at the intersection, swing the yarn in the right hand out and around the bottom, and up and over the tip of the right needle. Take right needle in right hand (Fig. 3c–3d).

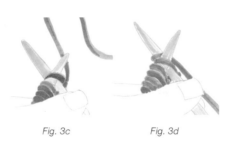

Fig. 3c   Fig. 3d

5. Using your right hand to steer the needle, hook the new strand of yarn you just made, taking the right needle back out of the loop (Fig. 3c–3f). Now there's one new stitch on your right needle.

Fig. 3e   Fig. 3f

6. Pull the right needle away from the left, sliding the left stitch off its needle (Fig. 3g). You have just knitted a stitch (Fig. 3h). Now, repeat steps 3–7 until there are no more stitches on the left needle.

Fig. 3g   Fig. 3h

7. To begin a new row, switch hands so the needle with the stitches is held in your left hand and the empty needle is held in your right hand. The row just completed is always on the left hand and the right hand needle always does the work. Now you can start the whole process over again.

Step 7 also applies after you stop and put down your needles when you are knitting in the middle of a row. To begin knitting again, the side where your ball of yarn is joined should be held in your right hand.

PURL STITCH

If you know the knit stitch well enough to do it upside down, you're ready to learn the purl stitch. The purl stitch is the knit stitch upside down.

Note: For both knitting and purling, when you wrap the yarn to make a new stitch you use the same way of wrapping.

1. Before you begin to purl, you need to put the yarn from the ball end into position. You do this by bringing the strand of yarn toward you and on top of the right needle.

2. Looking at the first loop, remember where you threaded the needle when you did the knit stitch. To purl, thread the empty needle in the opposite direction (Fig. 4a). Instead of entering the loop from the underside of the needle, enter from the top. In other words, your needle goes out the knitting "in" direction and in the "out" direction (Fig. 4b).

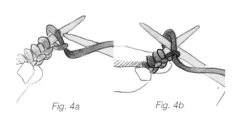

Fig. 4a   Fig. 4b

3. With your left hand supporting the crossed needles, wrap the yarn up, under and around the top/right needle exactly the same way as wrapping the yarn for the knit stitch (Fig. 4c–4d).

Fig. 4c   Fig. 4d

4. With your right hand returning to its original position, hook the right needle down and back out of the loop (Fig. 4e). Remember to bring the new loop you just created along for the ride (Fig. 4f).

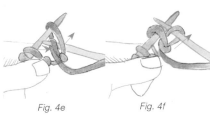

Fig. 4e   Fig. 4f

5. Drag the old loop off the left needle (Fig. 4g–4h).

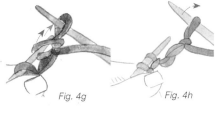

Fig. 4g   Fig. 4h

6. Now repeat steps 2–5. Your yarn is already in position after the first purl.

At the end of the row, change hands. If you are going to purl again, remember to put the yarn into position. The yarn has a tendency to hang down and put you in a knit position.

TENSION

Tension refers to how tight or loose your stitches are in relation to your needles. We strive for an even tension so that the stitches all look the same and the fabric is smooth. However, as a beginner, you want to strive to be a loose knitter. In other words, your stitches are not looped so tight on your needles that you have difficulty sliding the stitches across them.

The tension is controlled by how you hold the yarn from the ball end in your right hand. Wrapping the yarn around a couple of fingers may give you a better grip on the strand of yarn. I wrap the yarn around my pinky.

Whichever way you decide to hold the yarn, there's absolutely no need to do extra tugging after you've knitted a stitch because the stitches seem loose on the needles. To knit, you need to be able to have two needles fit into one stitch, and if the stitch is snug around the one needle, it will be difficult to insert the second needle. If your stitches are too tight, your needles will squeak in protest and knitting will be impossible.

Even tension makes even and uniform stitches, and comes with practice. Relax. Let your hands do the work.

KNIT AND PURL COMBINATIONS

When I refer to combinations of knits and purls in this section, I am not referring to the stocking stitch pattern, which you'll learn about later. Instead,

I'm referring to changing from knitting to purling and vice versa in the same row.

I recommend that you make sure you are quite comfortable with both the knit and purl stitches before attempting the combination. It will take some concentration.

To start, begin the row like any other. Then, once you have done the required stitches one way (either by knitting or purling), you need to change the yarn position before you do the stitches the other way.

Here's an example:

To start a row, knit five stitches. Then open the needles so that they are not touching each other, but not so far that the stitches are being pulled off the tips. Take the strand of yarn, swing it to the side facing you. The yarn is now in position for you to purl the next five stitches. After purling five stitches, separate the needles again and swing the yarn to the back to be in position to start knitting.

When doing combinations of knits and purls in the same row, remember to always put the yarn in position before doing the stitch. In other words, before starting the knit stitch, you need to put the yarn between the needles to the back. Before starting the purl stitch, you need to put the yarn between the needles to the front.

A Note on "Sides"

Throughout the book, you'll notice references to different "sides" of the piece you're working on. In knitting, the term "side" can mean different things depending on the context.
In my instructions, the **left** side is whatever you are holding in your left hand, and the **right** side is whatever you are holding in your right hand. Technically, these would be the left stitches and the right stitches.

Side also refers to the **front side** and the **back side** of the fabric you have knitted. The front side refers to the side of the fabric that is facing you while you are knitting, the back side refers to the side that is facing away from you.

In this book, whenever it says left or right, it means from your vantage point while you're holding the needles—your left and your right.

Finally, there are sides to a finished piece. The right side, usually abbreviated as **RS**, is the side of the piece that, when finished, everyone sees. The wrong side, usually abbreviated as **WS**, is the side of the piece that, when finished, is against the body.

To keep track of where you are in the knitting process, many patterns will identify which side you should be working on.

Many knitting projects are garments made up of multiple pieces and are described in relation to how you wear it.

Front – the piece that makes the front of the garment.
Back – the piece that makes the back of the garment.
Right – right front or right sleeve—can be the right side of a cardigan, your right sleeve or just a piece that is on the right side of the garment. Just remember the right refers to the pieces on your right side when you are wearing it.
Left – left front or left sleeve—can be the left side of a cardigan, *your* left sleeve or just a piece that is on the left side of the garment.

And then there's the instance when a pattern may instruct you to sew up your sides, referring to the side seams of your garment.

READING YOUR WORK

Knitting seems to be a lot of counting and concentration. But in fact, if you know how to read your work, you don't have to keep count! Reading your work is easy to do by looking at your stitches.

If you look at the stitch on your left needle, the stitch just about ready to be completed, you will see the loop on the needle standing up and down. Now look at the base of the up and down loop. Is the base a half "v" or a bump?

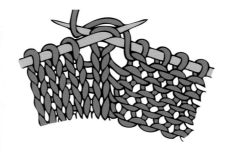

If the base is a half "v," then you should knit the stitch. If the base of the loop is a bump, you should purl the stitch. If a pattern says, "knit the stitches as they present themselves", it means knit the "v's" and purl the bumps. This is easy to remember, because if you look at the letter "k" for knit, the letter is made up of two "v's". If you look at the letter "p" for purl, the letter has a bump. ·

This is, of course, a general rule. But sometimes you'll use a pattern where you'll have to do the opposite, for example, when you do the first row of the alternating checkerboard pattern (see page 25). In this case, you'll be doing the opposite of what the stitches read.

TURNING

Turning occurs when you are mid-row and you stop and change directions by switching hands. Instead of completing the row, the remaining stitches on the left needle take a break from knitting and the stitches just completed are worked on. In most cases, the stitches that are taking a break are transferred onto a stitch holder (see "Transferring Stitches" on page 19).

A lot of garment patterns have turning in the instructions. For a sweater, turning is used in making the neckline because you work one side of the neckline at a time.

Steps for turning:
1. Knit the number of stitches as instructed in the pattern.
2. Transfer the stitches from the left needle onto a stitch holder. Notice that the first stitch to be transferred is the stitch on the needle not attached to the ball of yarn.
3. Turn by switching hands. Continue working on this section as outlined in the pattern.

CASTING OFF

Sometimes called binding off, casting off is a way to close the stitches into a sort of braid so they don't unravel

1. At the end of the row, turn, and knit one stitch, then a second stitch. You should never have more than two stitches at one time on the right needle when casting off.

2. If you look at the two stitches on your right needle, identify the stitch closer to the tip of the needle as the front stitch and the stitch behind as the back stitch. Bring both stitches near the tip of the needle.

3. Hook the back stitch over the front stitch as when playing leapfrog. The back stitch leapfrogs over the front stitch and off the needle, and is "dropped."

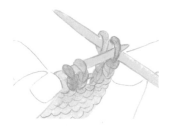

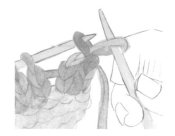

4. The back stitch has now been cast off.

5. Knit another stitch, and do the leapfrog process again. Repeat this until there are no stitches remaining on the left and only one stitch on the right.

6. You can now take your needle out of the last stitch. Pull the last stitch to make a giant loop by pulling the side of the stitch that pulls from the ball end of the yarn.

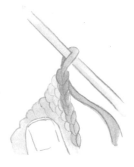

7. Cut yarn leaving a 4-inch (10 cm) tail.

8. Thread your strand of yarn through the loop you just made. Pull tight from the ball to close the loop.

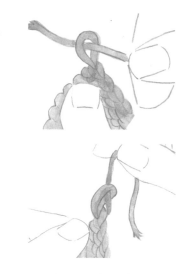

Loose stitches are best for casting off. The stitch not only has to be able to "jump over" the stitch in front of it, but it also has to span the width of the stitch in the cast-off seam. If you have a hard time to making your stitches looser, you can cast off using a larger diameter needle.

I usually tell my beginners to use the knit stitch for casting off, but you can also cast off in pattern. In other words, if you were doing ribbing, you would cast off in ribbing pattern.

Finishing

Finishing is a term used to describe the process of completing your project after all the knitting is done. It includes: blocking, assembling your piece, sewing it together, darning in the ends and adding embellishments.

BLOCKING

After knitting your pieces, the next step is to "block" them. This involves adding humidity to the fabric so that as the fabric dries, the stitches of the fabric relax to become smooth and even.

Start by pinning your piece to the desired finished size onto an ironing board or other flat surface. Your pattern will give you the correct sizes.

There are three ways to block your knitted fabric, from gentle on the fabric to the less so.

Blocking Methods:
a. Cover the fabric with a damp white cotton cloth and allow it to dry.
b. Spray a light mist of water on your fabric and allow to dry.
c. Hold a steam iron over your fabric without direct contact and shoot steam onto the surface. Allow to dry.

Once your fabric is dry from blocking, unpin it. You can now sew the pieces together.

SEWING

Most knitting projects will have pieces that need to be sewn together. Sewing takes time and a bit of practice, but extra care will ensure that your finished project will look just as nice as the knitted pieces.

To sew, you need a darning needle. The needle itself is actually not that much longer than a sewing needle; however, it has a very large eye, big enough to thread yarn through.

There are many ways to sew up your project. I prefer the "mattress stitch" method, and it's the method I use for 90% of my seams. The mattress stitch is done with the two right sides facing you and the seam you are working on in the middle. This method is the best because you can immediately see the seam you are creating.

How to sew up pieces using the mattress stitch.
1. Place the two knitted pieces to be sewn together face up and side by side, with the seam to be made positioned in the middle. Pin the pieces together at regular intervals so that they will line up as you sew.

2. Look at the direction of stitches on the pieces. Are you sewing:

> parallel pieces where the stitches on each piece run along the same direction

or

perpendicular pieces where the stitches run at a right angle to the other piece.

3. Based on the above observation, you will need to sew the pieces together as follows:

> For pieces with stitches running parallel vertically, if you separate the edge from the stitch next to it by gently pulling them apart, you'll see short horizontal strands. These strands are where your needle will weave the pieces together.
> For pieces with stitches running parallel horizontally, your needle will weave beneath the point of the "v" beneath each stitch.
> For pieces with stitches that are perpendicular, on the vertical piece of the knitting, your needle will weave in and out of the horizontal strands, and beneath the "v" points of the perpendicular piece.

4. Use either a tail of yarn that is a considerable length or a new piece of yarn. At the bottom of the pieces, thread the yarn into the darning needle.

5. Join the bottom corners together by looping the thread through the bottommost stitches a couple of times between the two edges to attach the corners together. This gives a good foundation to begin sewing.

6. To begin sewing, insert your needle under two of the strands according to the direction of the stitches in your first piece.

7. Then, move to the other piece and run your needle under the two parallel strands according to the direction of the stitches in that piece.

8. Back on the first side, weave your needle into the hole where you came out in step 6. Now pick up two more strands. Tug your thread snug to pull the two pieces together. Be careful not to pull too hard causing the seam to pucker or the yarn to break.

9. Continue to alternate sides, weaving between strands. Remember to enter the knitted piece where your needle came out the last time. You may need to adjust the number of strands you pick up on each side to keep the two pieces aligned.

10. Once you've finished sewing and pulling the pieces together, leave the end of the yarn dangling and darn it in later.

DARNING ENDS

Darning is when you tuck the "tails" of yarn into the fabric of the knitted piece. These ends are usually found at the beginning and the end of the piece. They are also found wherever you had to either cut or join the yarn. To darn the ends, you need a darning needle. Some needles come with tips that are bent. While a bent tip makes weaving the yarn easier, it's not necessary.

1. To darn in an end, take one of your "tails" and thread it one quarter way through the darning needle.

2. Now, looking at the fabric attached to the tail, pick an arbitrary knitted strand of yarn embedded in the fabric. Once you have chosen and identified your strand of yarn, that strand becomes the path for your tail.

3. With your darning needle, begin threading along your chosen path. The needle should be looping in and out of other loops, taking care to stay on the path. Basically, your tail is going to be hidden by following the strand into and amongst the fabric.

4. Darn in the tail as far along as possible. Once you have less than 1 inch (2.5 cm) left of the tail, cut the rest off.

Note: Some ends can be just darned into the seam. Others do not even need to be darned in. For example, the ends can be part of the fringe for a scarf, or just knotted together and made into a funky, decorative element. The ends may also have already been used for sewing the pieces together.

Beyond the Basics

READING A PATTERN

Having a pattern is very important to a beginner. A pattern for a knitting project is like a recipe for cooking a dish. A lot of people find reading knitting patterns like reading a foreign language. But once you know the language, It will be a piece of cake.

First of all, patterns are written in abbreviations. Like reading text messages on your phone from your friends, knitting patterns are written in a shorthand form. Once you become accustomed to the abbreviations, reading knitting patterns can be easy. See the back of this book for a list of the common knitting abbreviations you may come across.

VARIATIONS OF PATTERNS

Sometimes patterns appear different, depending on their source. Some patterns are abbreviated more than others. Monthly magazines tend to be the most abbreviated, whereas knitting books, especially those for beginners, have all the instructions written out in paragraph form. The patterns in this book will be in the middle of that continuum.

GUIDELINES TO READING A KNITTING PATTERN

Skill Level – A lot of the patterns indicate what knitting skill level is needed to knit the project, from beginner to experienced. I tell my students that while an advanced project will take more concentration and require more patience than a beginner project, the more passionate you are about a project the more likely you are to finish it. Go for it!

Sizes – A pattern may be written for multiple sizes, indicated by parentheses or brackets. For example, if a pattern includes three sizes—small, medium and large—it will be written as S [M, L].

Throughout the pattern, whenever you see numbers in square brackets [x, y], you'll know these numbers are for the different sizes. If you're knitting a medium size, you'll know that the number you always refer to is the number immediately after the first bracket. Your number will always be in the same position.

I suggest that before you even start knitting, go through the pattern and circle the number for the size you are knitting. You may think this is funny, but forgetfulness can happen, especially if you set your project down for an extended period of time!

Row Numbering – When I write patterns, I like to identify the rows by numbering them (e.g. Row 1, Row 2, etc). However, don't confuse these with the number of rows to be knitted. If the pattern says "Row 2: Knit," it means in the second row, you knit, not that you knit two rows.

Capitalization – When I first learned to read knitting patterns, I was confused with the difference between upper case "K" and lower case "k." For example, the pattern may read, "Row 43: K3, p2, k2, and p to the end." What I finally realized is that the first "k" is capitalized because it is at the beginning of the sentence, not because it is a different stitch!

Take note that some abbreviations are always capitalized. Like M1 for "make one."

Abbreviations – Although there is an industry standard for knitting abbreviations in patterns, always check the list included with the pattern so there is no misinterpretation.

Row Instruction Shorthand – There are two industry standards used to shorten row instructions. An asterisk (*) indicates a point in the instructions that gets returned to over and over again.

For example, "K4, *p3, k3, rep from the * until rem 4 sts, k4." Let's say, your needle had 26 stitches, then the instructions written out would look like this: K4, p3, k3, p3, k3, p3, k3, k4.

A pair of round brackets, ( ), usually contain a group of instructions that can be considered a unit.

For example, "P2, [k5, p5] two times, k20, (p5, k5) two times, p2." This instruction written completely would look like this: P2, k5, p5, k5, p5, k20, p5, k5, p5, k5, p2.

Stitch Count – At the end of the sentence, you may find a number or a group of numbers following the period. These numbers indicate the number of stitches that should be on your needle after completing that row. For example, "K6 [7,8], M1, k7, M1, k6 [7,8]. 21 [23,25] sts." This means you should have 21 stitches if you are knitting size small, 23 stitches for medium and 25 stitches for large.

Stitch count is usually included after a row where the pattern instructs you to increase or decrease the total stitches on your needle. I find that it's in the stitch count that you realize you

have either made a mistake in your knitting or there's an error in the pattern somewhere. Theoretically, the numbers should add up.

Photocopying – It is against copyright laws for knitters to photocopy patterns. You can only make a working copy so you don't have to write it out by hand or carry around your knitting book.

Finally, when in doubt, if you find the pattern instructions confusing, refer to the schematic drawings if they are included. If that doesn't work, examine the picture of the finished garment. Sometimes the picture shows you what the pattern designer is telling you to do.

KNITTING ON GAUGE

Once you've mastered knitting, you'll settle into your regular tension (see page 12 for a refresher) and discover if you're a loose, normal or tight knitter. I know I said to strive to knit loose, but you are who you are. However, regardless of whether you are a loose, normal, or tight knitter, you must knit your project on gauge for the pattern to turn out well.

"Knitting on gauge" means to knit the correct number of stitches to make up 4 inches of stitches. The reason this is important is because it will determine the finished size of the project. If you don't knit on the gauge the pattern is designed for, you will find that the fabric does not drape well or fit the person it was intended for. It will either be too loose if you are a loose knitter, or too tight if you are a tight knitter.

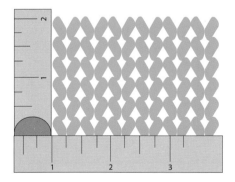

The good news is that if you are either a tight or a loose knitter, it is easy to adjust in order to knit on the gauge. You do not change your knitting—you knit the same and change the needle size.

Remember earlier in the book I mentioned that the manufacturer of the yarn indicates the recommended gauge of the yarn—how many stitches are knitted in stocking stitch over 4 inches (10 cm) with a particular size of knitting needles. For example, for a double knitting weight yarn, the ball band says using #6 (4 mm) needles will result in 22 stitches.

You discover when you use that needle size to knit the sample, you measure 20 stitches in the swatch (because you are a loose knitter). Make another sample gauge swatch using smaller needles. Try #5 (3.75 mm). You find with these needles you get the 22 stitches. Great! Use the that size needle for the project. Just remember to note the needle substitution in your pattern.

However, if you get 21 stitches, then you'll have to make a third sample swatch with the next smaller size needles, and so on.

How to knit a sample gauge swatch:

1. With the recommended needle size, cast on a few stitches more than the number indicated in the gauge.
2. Knit in the recommended stitch pattern (do not assume it is always in stocking stitch).
3. Knit until you have an approximate square.
4. Cast off loosely.
5. Measure the gauge with a ruler. The number of stitches per 4 inches (10 cm) will give you your gauge.

TRANSFERRING STITCHES ONTO A STITCH HOLDER

A stitch holder is a place to put aside stitches while still keeping them attached to the fabric of your work. Temporarily, the stitches are not worked on, but are still live loops that can be easily worked on later.

Many commercial stitch holders look like giant safety pins; however, any stick can work. You can use everyday objects like pencil crayons or chopsticks. Just make sure the diameter of the stick is not bigger than the loops and that the stitches do not slip off easily.

Hold the needle with the stitches that need transferring in your left hand, and the stitch holder with the open end touching the tip of the needle in your right hand.

Carefully slip the holder into the loops of the stitches on the end of your needle and pass them along until they are fully onto the holder. Reverse the process to put them back on your needle when you need to work them again.

CUTTING YOUR YARN AND THE END OF THE BALL

Once in a while your pattern will instruct you to cut your yarn. It's just as simple to do as it sounds. Just remember not to cut your yarn too close to the stitches. Always leave approximately 4 inches (10 cm) of yarn as a tail. You will need that for darning later.

What do you do when you have reached the end of your ball of yarn? There are two things to keep in mind: (1) You always need at least a 4-inch (10 cm) tail to darn in; (2) always join your yarn at the end of the row.

How do you know you have enough left for another row on the ball? Use this trick:

1. When you think you may be running low on yarn, take the remaining yarn and fold in half.
2. At the halfway point, mark the spot with a temporary knot.
3. Complete your row.
    If you find you have to go past the temporary halfway knot, untie it and complete the row. Then join a new ball of yarn (see "Joining Yarn" below). If you find that you do not get to the knot, there's still enough yarn for one or two rows. Untie the knot and go back to the first step.

JOINING YARN

To join a new ball of yarn, tie off the leftover yarn from the old ball so you don't accidentally use it again. Then, while leaving a 4-inch (10 cm) tail end from the new ball, just start knitting with the new ball of yarn. It's that simple.

Remember, you should be at the edge of your piece. Try not to join yarn in the middle of the row, unless instructed.

INCREASING

Sometimes, when you are knitting a piece, the pattern asks you to increase the total number of stitches on the needle. Increasing is a way to change the shape of your fabric.

There are a few ways to increase stitches; I'm going to describe both the "make one" and "yarn over" methods.

Make One

Make one (abbreviated as M1) is an almost-invisible method to add a stitch. It is created using the following steps:

1. At the point where you want to make one stitch, open your needles apart. You can see that the stitches are joined by a row of yarn rungs, like the rungs on a ladder.
2. With your left needle, hook the top rung, in the direction from the front to the back. This makes a new loop on your left needle.
3. Using your right needle, knit stitch from the back of the loop. You have just made a stitch.

Yarn Over

Yarn over (abbreviated as Yo or yo) is a decorative method of increasing. Yarn over not only increases your overall stitches, but also creates a hole in the fabric. A series of yarn overs creates a lace pattern. Yarn over is literally a strand of yarn looped over the needle. To make this, you deliberately put your yarn in the wrong position before you knit or purl. For example, if you are knitting, a yarn over is made by the following steps:

1. Knit until you are at the place where you want your hole.
2. Open your needles; place your yarn in front as if to purl.
3. Knit the next stitch. A loop is created. This loop is treated as a stitch in your next row.

Note: The act of putting the yarn looping over the needle is the yarn over. Yo "stitch" does not include the knit/purl stitch immediately after.

DECREASING

On the other hand, sometimes the pattern asks you to decrease the total number of stitches on the needle. Decreasing, like increasing, is another way to change the shape of your fabric.

There are a few variations for decreasing stitches. I am going to describe the "knit two together" and the "purl two together" methods.

Knit Two Together

Knit two together (abbreviated as K2tog or k2tog) is just what it says it is. Your right needle literally takes two stitches from the left together, and you knit them into one stitch.

How you do this:
1. With your right needle, you skip over to the second stitch from the end of the left needle.
2. You insert your right needle into the second, then the first stitch on the left needle.
3. Then, you knit them together.

Conversely, purl two together (abbreviated as P2tog or p2tog) is taking two stitches as if to purl from the left together, and purling them into one stitch.

How to do this:
1. Insert right needle into the first and second stitches of the left needle.
2. Purl them together.

After a row of increasing or decreasing stitches, always count the number of stitches on your needle. This number should correspond to the number of stitches indicated at the end of the row instructions in the pattern.

CASTING ON MID-ROW
Backward Loop Method (BWLM)
Sometimes you need to add multiple stitches to your fabric at the end of a row or mid-row. This creates an extra piece of fabric on one edge of the shape of your piece.

To cast on mid-row, you usually use the backward loop method:
1. Begin at the end of your row when all the stitches are on the right needle.
2. Keep the needle on your right.
3. Then take the yarn from the ball and make a loop by twisting toward the right.
4. Hook that loop onto the end of the right needle.
5. You have just cast on a stitch. Repeat steps 3 and 4 until you have the desired number.

BUTTONHOLE
There are two methods for making buttonholes: one is the "yarn over one stitch" buttonhole (sometimes called the round buttonhole), and the other is the "multiple stitch horizontal" buttonhole.

One Stitch Buttonhole
Makes a round buttonhole and is basically the creation of an eyelet in the fabric. This method is a one-row process. In other words, you only deviate from your knitting pattern in one row.

To create this buttonhole, you use a combination of two stitches, an increasing stitch, yarn over (yo), and a decreasing stitch. The decreasing stitch can be either knit two together (k2tog) or purl two together (p2tog), depending on what your knitting pattern dictates.

For example, the pattern would read: "Row 5: K5, yo, k2tog, k56."

Multiple Stitch Horizontal Buttonhole
This makes a horizontal slot in the fabric for the button to go through and is used when the button is bigger.

Creating this buttonhole is a two-row process and requires you to deviate from your knitting pattern for two rows. In the first row, you cast off the required stitches mid-row. Then in the second row, you cast the stitches back on using the BWLM method.

For example, the pattern for a stocking stitch (st st) fabric on the knit side would be:
"Row 5: K5, cast off 2 sts, k56.
Row 6: P56, cast on 2 sts using BWLM, P5."

Casting Off a Partial Row

When you are casting off a partial row, you actually have to knit or purl one more stitch so you can cast off the last number of stitches required. For example, if you have to cast off 14 stitches, you have to knit the 15th stitch so that the 14th stitch can "leap frog" (see "Casting Off on page 14") over and off the needle.

Note: The third buttonhole type is the "Multiple Stitch Vertical" Buttonhole which is a miniature keyhole (see "Part Five – Keyhole" on page 26).

DESIGN
A Note on Stitches

When we talk about stitches in knitting, we can refer to a number of different things. Stitches can be the number of loops on your needles. A knit stitch is when you knit a single stitch and a purl stitch is when you purl a stitch. Patterns made in the fabric are also commonly called stitches, for example the stocking stitch or garter stitch.

STITCH PATTERNS
Garter Stitch (G st, g st)

The garter stitch pattern is made by knitting every stitch for every row. It can also be made by purling every stitch for every row. Most knitters knit rather than purl to make the garter stitch. This is the easiest pattern for knitting and is used for almost all beginner scarves. The stitch looks the same on both sides and lies flat.

Garter Stitch

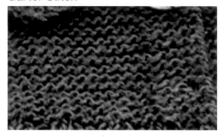

Stocking Stitch (St st, st st)

The stocking stitch is made when you alternate between knit and purl rows (i.e., knit one whole row, purl one whole row, knit one whole row, etc.). Stocking stitch pattern is most commonly seen in sweaters, whether they are hand knitted or machine knitted. If you look really closely on any T-shirt fabric, you'll notice it is usually in stocking stitch.

Although knit one row and purl one row is called stocking stitch, it usually refers to the side of the fabric that is flat, smooth and a series of repeating "v's". Some would refer it as the "knit side." The other side of the knit one row and purl one row is called reverse stocking stitch.

Stocking Stitch

Reverse Stocking Stitch (reverse st st)

Just as it says, this is the other side of the stocking stitch. It is made when you alternate between knit and purl rows (Fig. 5d). It refers to the side of the fabric that is bumpy. Some would refer it as the "purl side."

Fig. 5d Reverse Stocking Stitch

Rib Stitch (Rib, rib)

The rib stitch consists of alternating between knits and purls in the same row. You may have already heard the saying "knit one, purl one." This phrase is describing the 1 x 1 rib, in which you alternate between the knit stitch and the purl stitch in the same row.

Other rib patterns can include: 2 x 2 rib (Fig. 5b) alternating between k2 and p2, 3 x 3 rib alternating between k3 and p3, etc. Some ribs can be made asymmetrical by alternating between k3 and p2.

In reading pattern, you should know that some patterns mean "rib" as a stitch. It just means that you follow the ribbing pattern for as many stitches as indicated and then do whatever stitch it instructs. For example, you may see the following:

Rib 3, (M1, rib 5) 6 (7, 8) times, M1, rib 3. 43 (49, 55)sts.

When knitting the rib stitch, be sure your knits and purls line up. This stitch really allows you to practice reading your work. For example, 1 x 1 rib (knit 1, purl 1) doesn't necessarily start every row with a knit. If you have an uneven total number of stitches on your needle, one row will start with a knit and the next will start with a purl.

Usually ribbing is used as the welt at the bottom edge of a sweater. It provides a stretchy foundation for the sweater and for the cuffs of the sleeves. The rib helps the sweater to hold its shape. The rib pattern also makes great scarves. Ribbing has a great stretch factor and always lies flat.

If you are making a rib stitch scarf, keep in mind that ribbing takes up more yarn and has a tendency to shrink narrower than when you first knit it. In other words, design it wider than you intend to allow for the shrinking.

Fig. 5b Rib Stitch

Seed or Moss Stitch Pattern

The seed (or moss) stitch pattern is very similar to the rib stitch pattern, except that the knits and purls don't line up. You are basically making a miniature textured checkerboard pattern by alternating knits and purls.

This pattern can be used as the welt for sweaters and makes great scarves. It also makes great baby blankets and washcloths.

There is an amazing array of stitch pattern possibilities with the combination of only knit and purl stitches.

STITCH CALCULATION

Now that you've decided to design your own knitted masterpiece, the simplest thing to design is a scarf. Once you've decided on a yarn, needle size, and stitch pattern, how many stitches do you need to cast on to your needles?

Begin as you do for all projects by knitting a sample gauge swatch (see page 19). Measure your gauge and write that number down.

Let's say you have 12 stitches in 4 inches (10 cm), here's how you figure out how many stitches you cast on for a scarf 6 inches (15 cm) wide. Think back to math class and use cross multiplication:

12 sts x 6 in ÷ 4 in = 18 sts
or
12 sts x 15 cm ÷ 10 cm = 18 sts

Voila! You need to cast on 18 stitches for your scarf.

Tip

Stocking stitch makes terrible scarves. As you knit the fabric you will find that the whole thing will curl on the sides. No matter how well you block it, the scarf will always revert to curling. However, if you like the look of the knit side for your scarf, you can knit a double wide scarf, sew it into a tube, and then block it flat to prevent it from curling.

Knit A Scarf

A scarf is a great first project because it's simple and useful. Rather than simply knitting a long rectangle of fabric, this scarf gradually takes you to more complicated stitches. It gives you a more refined look.

materials

Approx. 110 yd (100 m) worsted-weight yarn
US 9 (5.5 mm) straight needles
Stitch holder
Gauge: 17 sts = 4 inches (10 cm) in st st

PART ONE - LEARN TO KNIT:
Cast on 26 sts.
Knit in garter stitch (knit all stitches and rows) until fabric forms a square. If you don't have a ruler handy, just fold the scarf along the diagonal. When the sides are the same length, you've got a square.

PART TWO -
INTRODUCTION TO PURL:
Row 1: Knit.
Row 2: Knit.
Row 3: Purl.
Repeat the three rows listed above 10 more times (if you include the first, then the total is 11 times or 33 rows).
Row 34: Knit.

PART THREE - COMBINATION KNITS AND PURLS:
The row pattern is as follows: k7, p6, k6, p7. Repeat for 8 rows. Then: p7, k6, p6, k7. Repeat for 8 rows. Repeat the last 16 rows one more time, making a 4 column x 4 row checkerboard pattern.

PART FOUR - RIBBING:
Row 1: *K1, p1*, repeat from * to *, to the end of the row.
Knit the rib pattern for 7 more rows, for a total of 8 rows of ribbing.

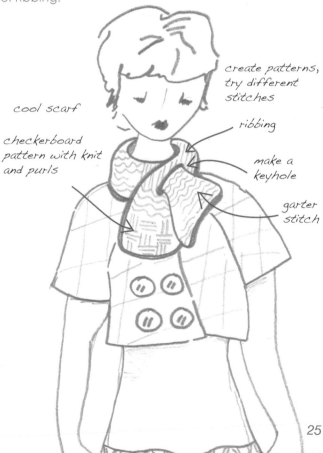

create patterns, try different stitches

cool scarf

ribbing

checkerboard pattern with knit and purls

make a keyhole

garter stitch

PART FIVE - KEYHOLE:

Row 1: (RS) *K1, p1*, repeat from * to * until you have 13 sts on the right needle. Place the stitches on the other needle onto a stitch holder (which will be identified as stitch holder #1).

Then turn (switch hands) and only work on one side of the scarf.

Row 2: (WS) *P1, k1*, repeat from * to * the end of the row.

Repeat the first and second rows 5 times each, then Row 1 once more, ending with the RS.

Cut yarn, leaving a 4 in/10 cm tail. Place the 13 sts you've just finished working on to another stitch holder (identified as stitch holder #2). Transfer stitches from stitch holder #1 back onto the empty needle. Join yarn and rib for 11 rows, as for the first side, ending on the outside edge.

Note: Making a mini keyhole is basically the creation of a vertical buttonhole.

PART SIX - THE END:

To join up the keyhole, start from the outside edge of your panel, rib for one row.

Then at the end of the row for that panel, at the center of the scarf, join and rib a row onto the other panel.

Part 2: Introduction to Purl

Part 3: Combination Knit and Purl

Part 5: The Keyhole

To do this, you must do the following steps:

1. At the outside of the last panel you were working on, rib one row to the center of the scarf.

2. You should now have a needle with stitches just completed and an empty needle.
Transfer the stitches from stitch holder #2 onto the empty needle.
Make sure that center end of the panel is closest to the point of the needle. If not, transfer again to flip over the stitches.

3. Put the work that is attached to the yarn in your right hand and the needle with the newly transferred stitches in your left hand.

4. Rib the transferred stitches.

5. You have now joined the scarf back together again.

Continue ribbing for 8 more rows. Then garter stitch 8 more rows. Cast off.

COUNTING ROWS

Counting the number of rows you have knitted can be tricky. Of course, you can keep track of the number of rows while you knit them either with pencil and paper or with a row-counter device.

However, sometimes you need to look at your knitted fabric and count the rows. Keep in mind that your cast-on row does not count as a row. Your first row is the row right above it. For garter stitch, your second row is actually on the other side of the fabric. So on the one side, for garter stitch you see every other row. A row looks different depending on what stitch pattern you are knitting.

Slouch Hat

This style of hat is very hot right now, and works on both guys and girls. Experiment with different colors and textures of yarn to complement your own look.

materials

Approx. 165 yd (150 m) worsted weight yarn
US 9 (5.5 mm) straight needles
Darning needle
Gauge: 17 sts = 10 cm/4 inches

Cast on 92 sts. You will need at least 2 both arm lengths of yarn tail to cast on. The stitches will be squished on the needle, but that is acceptable.

K1, p1 rib until hat measures 1.5 in/4 cm.
Next row (RS): K10, (yo, k18) four times, yo, k10. (97 sts)
Next row(WS): Purl.
St st until hat measures 8.5 in/22 cm total (including the rib).

Drop Stitches Row (RS): K10, (drop 1 st, k18) four times, drop 1 st, k10.
Next Row (WS): Purl.

slouches nicely at the back

play with colors and textures – create your own look!

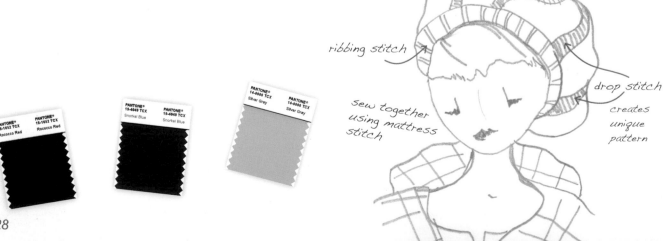

ribbing stitch

drop stitch

sew together using mattress stitch

creates unique pattern

28

CROWN

Row 1 (RS): K8, (k2tog, k7) nine times, k2tog, k1. (82 sts)
Row 2 (WS): P1, (p2tog, p6) nine times, p2tog, p7. (72 sts)
Row 3: K6, (k2tog, k5) nine times, k2tog, k1. (62 sts)
Row 4: P1, (p2tog, p4) nine times, p2tog, p5. (52 sts)
Row 5: K4, (k2tog, k3) nine times, k2tog, k1. (42 sts)
Row 6: P1, (p2tog, p2) nine times, p2tog, p3. (32sts)
Row 5: K2, (k2tog, k1) nine times, k2tog, k1. (22 sts)
Row 6: P1, (p2tog) ten times, p1. (12sts)
Row 7: (K2tog) six times. (6 sts)

With 6 sts left on the needle, cut yarn, leaving a
4 in/10 cm tail. Draw yarn through remaining 6 sts,
starting with the loop at the back of the needle, and
pull tight to close the top of the hat. Thread through
center of hat.

Sew the hat together using the mattress stitch. Darn ends.

DROP STITCH

A drop stitch is made when you insert the right
needle into the next stitch as if to knit, but
instead slide the stitch off the left needle and
let it fall, creating a run down the fabric of
your piece."

Ribbed Tube Top

This cute top looks great on its own or buttoned to the accompanying shrug (see pattern on page 32). You can choose to knit it in the same color or a different color from the shrug to mix and match.

materials

Approx 440 yd (400 m) worsted-weight yarn
US 9 (5.5 mm) straight needles
Gauge: 23 sts = 4 inches (10 cm) over
 rib pattern, slightly stretched

SIZES

The sizes; X-Small (Small, Medium, Large)
To fit bust: 30 in (32-34, 36-38, 40-42 in) or
76 cm (81-86, 92-97, 100-107 cm)

Actual Knitted Circumference:
21 in (24, 27, 30 in)
53 cm (61, 67, 76 cm)

part of the "shrug sweater set"

tube top - ribbing stitch

sew upsides with mattress stitch, insert elastic band to top edge

add buttons so it can be attached to the shrug cardigan

big wooden buttons, two front, two back

TUBE

Make two.

Cast on 62 (70, 82, 90) sts.

Row one (RS): *K2, p2, repeat from *, k2.

Row two (WS): *P2, k2, repeat from *, p2.

Repeat rows one and two to make the 2 x 2 rib pattern.

Continue in 2 x 2 rib pattern until tube top measures 14 in/36 cm or to your desired length, ending with a WS row.

(RS): Purl one row to create a fold line for elastic band top.

(WS): *P2, k2, repeat from *, p2.

Continue in 2 x 2 rib pattern until elastic band casing measures 1.25 in/3 cm ending with a WS row.

Cast off loosely.

Finishing

Sew up the sides. On one side, leave elastic band casing open to insert elastic.

Fold and sew down elastic band casing.

Insert 1-inch-wide elastic and sew in.

Darn ends and block.

Sew buttons for Shrug Cardigan.

SHRUG + TUBE TOP = SWEATER

Top-Down Shrug Cardigan

materials

Approx 440 yd (400 m) worsted-weight yarn
US 9 (5.5 mm) needles
Buttons: 3
Gauge: 17 sts = 4 inches (10 cm) over gs

SIZES

X-Small (Small, Medium, Large)
To fit bust: 30 (32-34, 36-38, 40-42 in) or
76 (81-86, 92-97, 100-107 cm)

.
Actual Knitted Circumference: 28 (32, 38, 41) in or 71
(81, 96, 104) cm

Note: For this garment you are knitting top down. In other words, you start at the collar and work your way down to the ribbing at the bottom. Please read the pattern in its entirety before beginning.

LEFT SIDE

Cast on 36 sts.
(RS) Purl one row.
Beginning with WS row, knit in garter stitch pattern (knit all rows) until collar measures 5.5 in/15 cm ending with a WS row.

Note: With garter stitch, it's hard to differentiate between the RS (Right Side) and the WS (Wrong Side). I suggest that you place a safety pin on the RS of the piece, so that whenever the side with the safety pin is facing you, you know that you are knitting the RS.

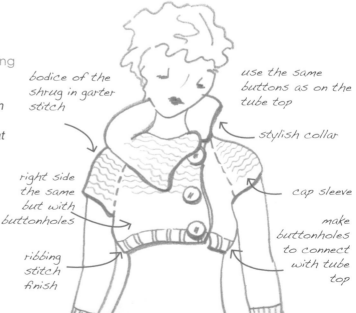

bodice of the
shrug in garter
stitch

use the same
buttons as on the
tube top

stylish collar

right side
the same
but with
buttonholes

cap sleeve

make
buttonholes
to connect
with tube
top

ribbing
stitch
finish

SHAPE SHOULDER / MARK SLEEVE

To begin shoulder shaping and formation of the sleeve, with RS facing you and in your left hand, attach a marker on the 2nd stitch and another one on the 9th stitch from the left tip of your needle. Use a safety pin, or something similar, and physically attach it to the actual stitch. Counting from left to right, you should have 1 st, 1 marked st, 6 sts, 1 marked st and 27 sts.

Row 1 (RS): K1, M1, k1 (marked stitch), M1, k6, M1, k1 (marked stitch), M1, k27. (40 sts).
Row 2 and subsequent even rows (WS): Knit.
Row 3: K2, M1, k1 (marked stitch), M1, k8, M1, k1 (marked stitch), M1, k28. (44 sts).

Note: Because the markers are actually attached to the stitch, the markers stay in the row you first placed them. While knitting the RS, transfer the marker up to the stitch on that row.

Continue with the shoulder shaping and formation of the sleeve, increasing on the RS rows with M1 on either side of the two marked stitches for 30 (38, 50, 58) rows (96 [112,136,152] sts).

Last increase row.

Row 31 (39, 51, 59): K16 (20, 26, 30), M1, k1 (marked stitch), M1, k36 (44, 56, 64), M1, k1 (marked stitch), M1 and k42 (46, 52, 57) [100 (116, 140, 156) sts].
Next row (WS): Knit.
Knit in garter stitch for 8 more rows ending with WS row. Remember to keep moving the markers up your rows.

JOIN BODICE / CREATE SLEEVE

(RS): K17 (21, 27, 31), k1 (marked stitch), cast off 38 (46, 58, 66), k1 (marked stitch), and k43 (47, 53, 57) (62 [70, 82, 90] sts). This is the total number of stitches on the needle, although it is divided up in two sections.

Markers can now be removed.

(WS): K44 (48, 54, 60), tighten up the stitches and join to next section, then k18 (22, 28, 32) for (62 [70, 82, 90] sts).

2 X 2 RIB

Row 1 (RS): *K2, p2, repeat from *, k2.
Row 2 (WS): *P2, k2, repeat from *, p2.
Repeat the above two rows to make the 2 x 2 rib pattern. Continue in 2 x 2 rib pattern until ribbing measures 1 inch (2.5 cm). End on a WS row.

OPTIONAL *(this is to connect the shrug to the tube top).*
Button hole row (RS): Rib 10 (14, 20, 24), cast off 2 sts, rib 12, cast off 2 sts, rib 36 (40, 46, 50). (58 [66, 78, 86] sts).
Next row (WS): Rib 36 (40, 46, 50), cast on 2 sts using backward loop method, rib 12, cast on 2 sts, use backward loop method, rib 10 (14, 20, 24). (62 [70, 82, 90] sts).

Continue in 2 x 2 rib pattern until total ribbing measures 2 in/5 cm ending with a WS.

Cast off loosely in the k2, p2 pattern.

Leave a very long end for sewing later and cut yarn.

RIGHT SIDE

Exactly like the left side, except with buttonholes. Cast on 36 sts.
(RS) Purl one row.
Beginning with WS row, knit in garter stitch pattern (knit all rows) until collar measures 5.5 in/15 cm ending with a WS row.

SHAPE SHOULDER / MARK SLEEVE

To begin shoulder shaping and formation of the sleeve, with RS facing you and in your left hand, attach a marker on the 2nd stitch and another one on the 9th stitch from the left tip of your needle. Use a safety pin or something similar and physically attach it on the actual stitch. Counting from left to right, you should have 1 st, 1 marked st, 6 sts, 1 marked st and 27 sts.

Row 1 and first buttonhole (RS): K1, M1, k1 (marked stitch), M1, k6, M1, k1 (marked stitch), M1, k24, cast off 2 sts, k1. (38 sts)
Row 2 (WS): K1, cast on 2 sts using the backward loop method, knit to the end. (40 sts)
Row 3: K2, M1, k1 (marked stitch), M1, k8, M1, k1 (marked stitch), M1, k28. (44 sts).

Row 4 and subsequent even rows (WS): Knit.
Continue with the shoulder shaping and formation of the sleeve, increasing on the RS rows with M1 on either side of the two marked stitches for 18 (24, 30, 34) rows. (72 [84,96,104] sts).

Place second buttonhole.
Row 19 (25, 31, 35): K11 (14, 17, 19), M1, K1 (marked stitch), M1, K26 (32, 38, 42), M1, K1 (marked stitch), M1, K34 (37, 40, 42), cast off 2 sts, K1. (74 [86, 98, 106] sts).
Row 20 (26, 32, 36): (WS): K1, cast on 2 sts using the backward loop method, purl to the end. (76 [88, 100, 108] sts).
Again, continue with the shoulder shaping and formation of the sleeve, increasing on the RS rows with M1 on either side of the two marked stitches. (96 [112,136,152] sts).

Last increase row. **Row 31 (39, 51, 59):**
K17 (21, 27, 31), M1, K1 (marked stitch), M1, K38 (46, 58, 66), M1, K1 (marked stitch), M1 and K43 (47, 53, 59) (100 [116, 140, 156] sts).
Next row (WS): Knit.

Knit in garter stitch for 8 more rows ending with WS row.

JOIN BODICE / CREATE SLEEVE
(RS): K17 (21, 27, 31), k1 (marked stitch), cast off 38 (46, 58, 66), k1 (marked stitch), and k43 (47, 53, 57). (62 [70, 82, 90] sts). This is the total number of stitches on the needle although it is divided up in two sections. Markers can now be removed.
(WS): K44 (48, 54, 60), tighten up the stitches and join to next section, then K18 (22, 28, 32) for 62 (70, 82, 90) sts.

RIB
Row 1 (RS): *K2, p2, repeat from *, k2.
Row 2 (WS): *P2, k2, repeat from *, p2.
Repeat the above two rows to make the 2 x 2 rib pattern.

Continue in 2 x 2 rib pattern until ribbing measures 1 in/2.5 cm ending with a WS.

Third buttonhole row (without optional buttonholes to connect with tube top) (RS):
Rib 59 (67, 79, 87), cast off 2 sts, rib 1. (60 [68, 80, 88] sts).

Next row (WS): Rib 1, cast on 2 sts using the backward loop method, rib 59 (67, 79, 87). (62 [70, 82, 90]).

OR
Third buttonhole with optional buttonholes to connect with tube top.

Button hole row (RS): Rib 10 (14, 20, 24), cast off 2 sts, rib 12, cast off 2 sts, rib 33 (37, 43, 47), cast off 2 sts, rib 1 (56 [64,76,84] sts).

Next row (WS): Rib 1, cast on 2 sts using the backward loop method, rib 33 (37, 43, 47), cast on 2 sts using the backward loop method, rib 12, cast on 2 sts using the backward loop method, rib 10 (14, 20, 24) (62 [70, 82, 90] sts).

Continue in 2 x 2 rib pattern until total ribbing measures 2 in/5 cm ending with a WS row.

Cast off loosely in the k2, p2 pattern.

FINISHING
On a table, with RS facing up, place the left side piece on the left and the right side piece on the right. Starting from the ribbing edge, using the mattress stitch, sew up to the base of the collar. Then flip work so that the WS is now facing up, and proceed to sew up the collar on the WS.

Darn ends and sew the three buttons on the left side edge.

PANTONE® 15-1239 TCX Cantaloupe
PANTONE® 15-1239TCX Cantaloupe

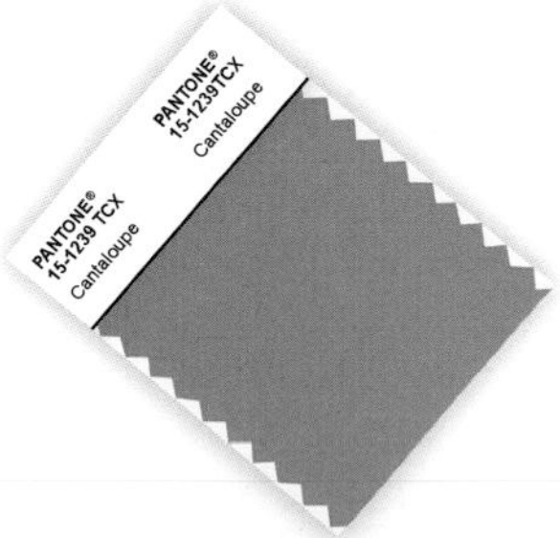

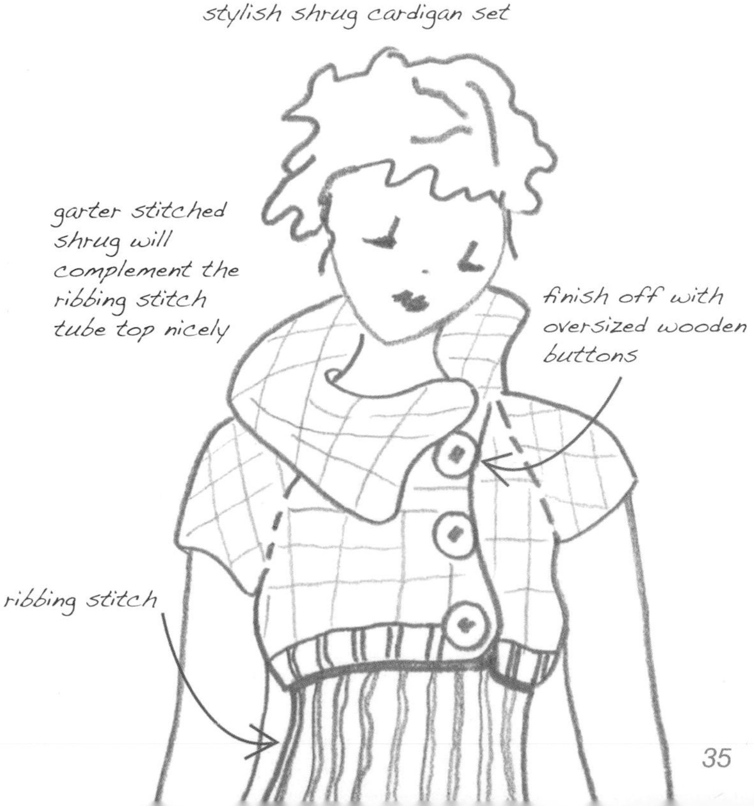

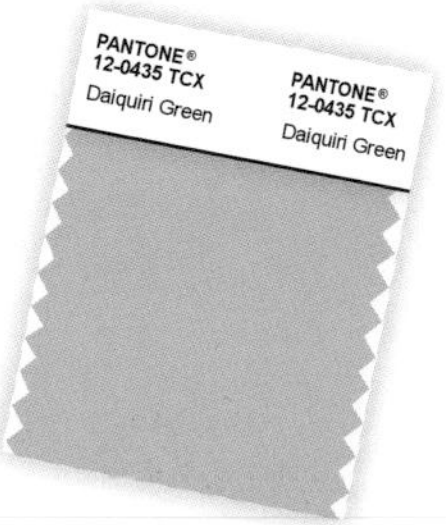

PANTONE® 12-0435 TCX Daiquiri Green
PANTONE® 12-0435 TCX Daiquiri Green

stylish shrug cardigan set
garter stitched shrug will complement the ribbing stitch tube top nicely
finish off with oversized wooden buttons
ribbing stitch

Appendix

Standard Yarn Weight System

Yarn Weight Symbol & Category Names	0	1	2	3	4	5	6
Type of Yarns in Category	Fingering 10-count crochet thread	Sock, Fingering, Baby	Sport, Baby	DK, Light Worsted	Worsted, Afghan, Aran	Chunky, Craft, Rug	Bulky, Roving
Knit Gauge Range* In Stockinette Stitch to 4 inches	33–40**sts	27–32sts	23–26 sts	21–24sts	16–20 sts	12–15 sts	6–11 sts
Recommended Needle in Metric Size Range	1.5–2.25mm	2.25–3.25mm	3.25–3.75mm	3.75–4.5mm	4.5–5.5mm	5.5–8mm	8mm and larger
Recommended Needle US Size Range	000–1	1–3	3–5	5–7	7–9	9–11	11 and larger
Crochet Gauge* Ranges in Single Crochet to 4 inch	32–42 double crochets**	21–32 sts	16–20 sts	12–17 sts	11–14 sts	8–11 sts	5–9sts
Recommended Hook in Metric Size Range	Steel*** 1.6–1.4mm	2.25–3.5mm	3.5–4.5mm	4.5–5.5mm	5.5–6.5mm	6.5–9mm	9mm and larger
Recommended Hook US Size Range	Steel*** 6,7,8 Regular hook B-1	B-1 to E-4	E-4 to 7	7 to I-9	I-9 to K-10 ½	K10 ½ to M-13	M-13 and larger

* GUIDELINES ONLY: The above reflect the most commonly used gauges and needle or hook sizes for specific yarn categories.

** Lace weight yarns are usually knitted or crocheted on larger needles and hooks to create lacy, openwork patterns. Accordingly, a gauge range is difficult to determine. Always follow the gauge stated in your pattern.

*** Steel crochet hooks are sized differently from regular hooks—the higher the number, the smaller the hook, which is the reverse of regular hook sizing.

Source: Craft Yarn Council of America's www.YarnStandards.com

ON KNITTING LEFT-HANDED
If you're a leftie, simply take the instruction in the knitting section and switch left with right, and flip the instructions by looking at them in a mirror.

ABBR.	DESCRIPTION
[ ]	work instructions within brackets as many times as directed
( )	work instructions within parentheses in the place directed
* *	repeat instructions following the asterisks as directed
*	repeat instructions following the single asterisk as directed
"	inches
alt	alternate
approx	approximately
beg	begin/beginning
bet	between
BO	bind off
CA	color A
CB	color B
CC	contrasting color
cm	centimeter(s)
cn	cable needle
CO	cast on
cont	continue
dec	decrease/decreases/decreasing
dpn	double pointed needle(s)
fl	front loop(s)
foll	follow/follows/following
g	gram
inc	increase/increases/increasing
k or K	knit
k2tog	knit 2 stitches together
kwise	knitwise
LH	left hand
lp(s)	loop(s)
m	meter(s)
M1	make 1 stitch
M1 p-st	make one purl stitch
MC	Main Color
mm	millimeter(s)
oz	ounce(s)
p or P	purl

ABBR.	DESCRIPTION
pat(s) or patt	pattern(s)
pm	place marker
pop	popcorn
p2tog	purl 2 stitches together
prev	previous
psso	pass slipped stitch over
pwise	purlwise
rem	remain/remaining
rep	repeat(s)
rev St st	reverse stockinette stitch
RH	right hand
rnd(s)	round(s)
RS	right side
sk	skip
skp	slip, knit, pass slipped stitch over; one stitch decreased
sk2p	slip 1, knit 2 together, pass slipped stitch over the knit 2 together; 2 stitches have been decreased
sl	slip
sl1k	slip 1 knitwise
sl1p	slip 1 purlwise
sl st	slip 1 stitch(es)
ss	slip stitch (Canadian)
ssk	slip, slip, knit these 2 stitches together; a decrease
sssk	slip, slip, slip, knit 3 stitches together
st(s)	stitch(es)
St st	stockinette stitch/stocking stitch
tbl	through back loop
tog	together
WS	wrong side
wyib	with yarn in back
wyif	with yarn in front
yd(s)	yard(s)
yfwd	yarn forward
yo	yarn over
yrn	yarn around needle
yon	yarn over needle

Glossary

BLOCKING – the process of moistening knitted pieces to relax the fibers and shape them into their final form before allowing them to dry. It ensures that all pieces are in the correct size and shape before sewing.

BOBBIN – a small plastic device around which yarn can be wrapped to prevent it from tangling.

CASTING OFF – the process of binding stitches to finish a piece of knitting; also called binding off.

CASTING ON – the process of beginning a piece of knitting by putting stitches on the knitting needles.

DARNING – used to hide the ends of yarn created by beginning, ending or changing yarn balls in the middle of a project; this involves weaving yarn between stitches so that it cannot be seen.

FINISHING – everything you need to do to complete a project after casting off, including blocking, assembly, sewing, darning and adding embellishments.

GARTER STITCH – the pattern achieved when you knit every stitch in every row.

GAUGE – the number of stitches per inch of knitted fabric used to measure yarn.

KNIT – the process of turning a strand of yarn or thread into fabric; refers to a particular stitch in knitting; stitches that look like "v's."

MOSS STITCH – a knitting pattern that results in a pattern of raised stitches resembling moss. The stitch is achieved by alternating knits and purls such that the stitches don't line up, resulting in a pebbly appearance.

PURL – the process of knitting that creates the inversion of the knit stitch; stitches that look like bumps.

RIB STITCH – a pattern of alternately knitting and purling such that the stitches line up and form a rib in the fabric.

SEED STITCH – another name for the moss stitch.

SKEIN – a quantity of yarn wound into a loose loop to prevent it from becoming tangled; skeins generally need to be wound into balls before knitting.

SLIP KNOT – a knot formed from a loop that allows for an increase or decrease in size.

STOCKING STITCH – the pattern achieved by alternately knitting and purling each row.

TENSION – this refers to how tight or loose your stitches are in relation to your needles; in knitting, strive for a tension that is even.

TRANSFERRING STITCHES – when turning, we generally transfer some stitches to a stitch holder, taking a break from knitting them further while still keeping them as part of the piece.

TURNING – occurs when you change direction in your knitting mid-row; essentially, you are taking a break from knitting some stitches.

How to Determine Your Size

As you've noticed, some of the patterns in this book come with sizes (X-Small, S, M, L). If you're not quite sure which size in which to knit your project, you can always measure. The most common areas to measure are the bust or chest, waist, underarm to wrist, and shoulder to wrist. These measurements will give you the best indication of which pattern size will work best for you. Once you've taken your measurements, select the size that is the closest. The bust or chest measurement is usually the most common indicator of size.

Note: You can measure either your body, or measure a garment whose fit you like to determine the right size for your project.

Here's how to measure each section. You'll need a measuring tape.

BUST/CHEST – with your tape, measure around the fullest section of the bust or chest.

WAIST – measure around the narrowest part of the midsection.

UNDERARM TO WRIST – on the inside of your arm, measure from your underarm crease to your wrist.

SHOULDER TO WRIST – on the outside of your arm, measure from shoulder bone to your wrist, while keeping arm slightly bent.